first

Kelli Dougal

Presentation by *BookLeaf Publishing*

Web: www.bookleafpub.com

E-mail: info@bookleafpub.com

ISBN: 9789360946173

First edition 2024

33 December 31sts

December 31 once meant
 sequined dresses,
 party poppers,
 midnight smooches,
 photo booths,
 fevered countdowns.
 once there was even a chocolate fountain.
Counting down to 12:00 together as a shrieking
mob,
delight in my eyes and glitter on my cheeks,
wondering in earnest if the next Dec 31 would
be spent with the same group of friends kissing
the same boy?
(spoiler: the friends stayed the same. the boys
usually changed.)

33 December 31sts.
One was spent in Shanghai
One was celebrated in Seoul
December 31sts have been had in
Boston and Miami and Dallas and Dayton, Ohio

But this year, on the
33rd December 31st,
I am going to bed early.
There's no Korean fried chicken or milk tea,

only the rainy and gray
Pacific Northwest
and my comfy bed who will cradle me while
12:00 quietly slips by,
unobserved.
I have kissed the same man for the last 6 years
and I have full confidence that he will be the one
I kiss a year from now.

At 6:30 pm I am snacking on cheese and sipping
Martinelli's, avoiding anything too greasy to try
keep myself from vomiting
(My body has decided that the "morning" in
"morning sickness" is open to interpretation)

There's no glitz,
just toddler spit stringy on my sweats
a yawn escapes.
my mother hustles around in the background,
trying to take care of me and everyone all at the
same time.

There's nothing exotic,
nothing exciting,
but as I watch my man toss that drooly boy in
the air,
spittle dripping from his chin as he giggles

there is something right

and maybe the
32 other December 31sts
were all just leading up to this one
when life would be quiet and comfy
and yet somehow
perfect.

(The less-than-perfect
EPILOGUE:
The "morning" sickness won
and the crab dip,
cream puffs,
and sparkling cider
made a less-than-ideal combination
coming back up.
Happy new year.)

restolution

isn't it odd
that the time of year we
humans have designated for
resolutions
resolves
renewal
is the time of year that
nature has designed for
rest

restolution part 2

5

no, really,
I think I'm onto something here.

what if we followed the wisdom of
the marmots and
the crocuses and
the black bears
instead of the suggestions of
life coaches and
marketers and
influencers and
whatever man in power decided the new year
began during the coldest month of the year?
(pope gregory xiii. he's the one to blame)

and what if
instead of
Forcing
our minds and bodies to
work out harder
eat smarter
be an earlier starter,
what if we just
Stopped

and

Listened

to our weary bodies
and our weary souls.

and what if we asked
what we needed-
really needed-
and offered it instead?
even if it meant
more naps and less reps.

I think nature might be onto something here.

mothers

retching, roiling,
heaving, sweating,
yellow bile pools up and out
trickling out the side of my grimacing mouth

sobbing "this is unfair"
"I don't want to do this"
"is there no other way?"

the vomiting hasn't stopped
even though my stomach is long empty.
my clothes are soaked with sweat as I tremble,
pale, against the porcelain

Brandon is on hold with the on-call doctor,
concerned about his spewing wife
-does she need the ER? does she need an IV?-
but no one is working on new years day

I breathe heavily, waiting for the next spasm
and my thoughts drift to our first mother.
Eve, the epitome of motherhood
the poster child for pregnancy.
at least we have an on-call doctor

and my mother-in-law downstairs distracting my
oblivious toddler.
who did she have?
when her body betrayed her
when the retching started
when the half-digested greens and grains pooled
around her in the dirt
what did she think?
who did she turn to?
did she think she was dying
did she regret her choice
as she looked around at her single support,
a worried but bewildered adam?

Surely her Mother reached out
a gentle caress of wind on her forehead
a sprinkle of rain to calm her fever
a whispered voice, "this too shall pass"
a vision of cherubic chubby baby toes to come
a promise of future joy beyond all she had
known,
offering small comforts during her moments of
pain and sacrifice that only another mother can
ever understand

Mother, I am not alone like Eve was
but in this moment, resting on my vomit-filled
bathtub,
I need you

I need that comfort, too
I need a reminder that I will make it through,
that these days of spilling my guts out around
me will end

There is no breeze in my bathroom,
no rain,
but the retching subsides for a moment,
enough that I can hear that small voice
"this will pass".

I am a mother
held up by generations of mothers.
I lift my head and wipe my mouth.
I will see this through.

God is not an old white man

God is not an old white man.
(I don't know many things,
but of this
I am certain).
He may have a beard, but it is
not merely long and white.
It is interweaved with every color of the
rainbow,
shimmering like mermaid scales and unicorn
hairs,
transcending the hues visible
to mortal eyes.
He is the wizened Cambodian monks in their
startlingly orange robes
She is the kind Korean mother who welcomed
me into her home and fed me kimchi,
transcending language with gestures that spoke
louder than my
two mispronounced words of Korean
She is the kind teacher who takes a special
interest in the child who shows up each day in
the same dirty sweatshirt
She is the abuelas in Miami who insisted on
feeding us missionaries until we couldn't move

(It was the old white men that yelled at us
because they knew everything and told us we
were wrong)
They are a Southern Baptist choir, worshiping
with every fiber in their being
She is the Polynesian mother embracing my
brother while he was away from his own mother
on his own mission
They are the spiritual guru in their ashram,
hoping to inspire others to find their own path of
enlightenment and live more simply
They are the humble street artist, painting
vibrant stories on city walls, turning concrete
into canvases that whisper tales to those who
pause to listen.

One day, we will see Them, and we will all find
ourselves surprised by Their face.
But none will be as surprised
As the old white men.

First

i.
I was first.
Shrieking and kicking and burbling,
I tumbled in
Never slowing down
especially not for the second.

Amusing, bossing, planning, plunging,
always leading the parade
as it expanded to a third, fourth, fifth

Eventually the bossing turned into
worrying
Protecting, defending, agonizing
Keeping the others safe.

Trying too hard, too much, too often

But I was First.
Reaching, achieving, expecting perfection
Forging, blazing, testing
Never allowed to slow down
or come in second.
This is the way of the Firsts.

ii.

And running ahead,
I did what was asked.
I pleased all the people.
I checked all the tasks.

But when I looked back,
I saw with dismay,
The others had struggled
While I'd found my way.

I hadn't been perfect
enough after all
To keep everyone stable
Or catch everyone's falls.

Did I fail in my role?
Did I do something wrong?
I will pick up the pieces
I'm the one who is strong

I will birth all the grandkids
I will not move away
I will take care of the parents
I will take care not to stray

I am the stable one
The strong link in the chain
I will support all my siblings
I will never complain—

iii.
I am still First.
and I am trying to
give myself all the grace
I held back over the years.

There is less bossing,
but still plenty of worrying
for the second, third, fourth, and fifth
and for the parents
But now I have my own family to
worry about.

Two firsts found each other
Both trying too hard
to stabilize our rocking families
at the expense of ourselves.
Two golden children
who did everything right
making sure all was well
for everyone else

Until we said
ENOUGH!

We are slowly healing
from the scars of the Firsts
as we gently let the burdens down

that we carried alone all this time

and we are surprised to find
that the others are okay.
maybe we could have let go a long time ago.

We are Firsts.
And we are rewriting what that means
as we raise our own little
first
without all the excess loads
we unnecessarily shouldered

my little first

You entered this world
like a hurricane,
no consideration of your due date,
water breaking at 3 AM
and announcing your arrival
with all the decorum of a freezing waterfall.

"I'm not ready," I whispered.
I wanted your arrival, my first,
to be perfect.

But perfect was not the plan.

In the chaos of a gray, rainy dawn,
our eyes wide with trepidation,
we pulled up, unprepared,
and when they asked for my birth plan
I squeaked out,
"To have this baby in six weeks…?!"

But oh, my darling,
you came when you wanted.
And you were perfect.

And I wanted to be the perfect mother
for you, my perfect, precious baby.

But
You are first
and this is my
first time trying motherhood
and we are figuring this out together,
one day at a time.

I hope you will forgive
the times I am wrong
the times I am impatient
the times I am less-than-sweet.
I promise I will forgive you, too.

Soon there will be a second.
And you will be the
perfect big brother
even if some days
you are wrong
or impatient
or less-than-sweet.

It will be our first time
with a second
and we will figure it out together,
one day at a time.

But you will always be
my little first,

my miniature hurricane,
the one who gave me
my most important title
and most treasured role.
Because of you,
I am a mother.

Guardian of Whispers

In the realm of tender hearts I tread;
To me the battle-worn children are led.
Bright-eyed whispers, worries unsaid,
All seeking comfort for the journey ahead.

Today's tale is not unlike others,
A child grieves the choices of fathers and
mothers.
I feel the weight of words not yet spoken
elsewhere
But this mystical room grants the power to
share.

I wait, and after a moment's stall,
Words bubble up, breaking the wall.
The shadow of divorce, heavy and near,
She wears a façade of strength, not a single tear.

Behind strong eyes, a sea of emotion,
Fear, hurt, confusion, a daughter's devotion.
My sweet girl, I wish I could say,
We'll mend this pain, let's find a way.

No magic wand, no spell to cast,
Only a presence, a role steadfast.

A fairy godmother in a therapist's guise,
I know listening is wherein the magic lies.

Soon the end comes, like a fairy-tale's fade,
She smiles, hopeful, no longer afraid.
No fix-all spell, just a comforting space,
To navigate the challenges she will face.

Children carry burdens, battles unfold,
And in this safe haven, their stories are told.
No grand enchantment, just a caring ear,
A magic woven in the moments here.

In this safe haven where healing is found,
I stand as guardian of this holy ground.
A beacon of solace, I have heard the plea;
I will keep guiding the young souls who come to
me.

Wander (from the archives)

(*Author's note: In college, I was a prolific poet and wrote dozens of poems, only to lose them all when my computer crashed at the end of my four years. I mourn the loss of those words. I recently rediscovered this poem in an email draft from 2012 and was so delighted to have this small glimpse into my 21-year-old self.*)

Am I selfish
for wanting to keep you close to me,
to keep you on a leash
while I wander a little longer?

Is it wrong of me
to hope that you will sit
to hope that you will stay
while I chase my dreams
just over that little hill?

If I promise to come back,
will you wait?

In my imagination,
I leave you at the top of this hill
as I venture down and around the next one

And you sit on that hill as the moon waxes
and as the moon wanes
and the sun never scorches you too much
because you are glad to wait.

And if I need to, I can look back at the hill
and see you on the top,
A beacon
beckoning me back to you
when my feet grow tired
and when I've discovered that this new hill
isn't much different from the one we were on.

But I know that my imagination lies.

Because you, too, are a wanderer

And I worry that if I leave you on that hill
you won't stay put
because you'll find other mounds to climb

And when I finally grow weary of wandering
I'll go back to my hill
only to find that you have grown weary of
waiting
and you are now sitting on some far, distant hill

and my hill is
empty

the ice storm (restolution part 3)

Overnight,
our road has been transformed into
a skating rink.
Our front lawn is frosted over
with glittering ice,
enticing but treacherous.
The first day, a few bold youngsters pull each
other in sleds they scrounged up from the
cobwebbed corners of their garage.
The next day, we watch as a bundled neighbor
unsuccessfully tries to scrape ice from his car,
eventually deciding his destination is not nearly
important enough.

On Tuesday, the neighborhood kids rejoiced, the
words "snow day" bouncing excitedly from
house to house.
Four snow days later, their groans at being stuck
inside echo around the city,
a city which has come to a halt.
Even the United States Postal Service
has foregone their motto
and given up on their appointed rounds.

Mother Nature has forced us all to stop.
Maybe She knows better than we do.

It all seems so timely,
since just days ago I reflected upon rest.

So I take this blessing in the spirit it is offered,
and we pause.
and we rest,
just like those
marmots and black bears.

And there is a change.
I can sense it.
I can't pinpoint it exactly,
but this week of slowing down
has done something refreshing for my soul
in a way that all those resolutions never did.

Nature just gets it.
And maybe I am one step closer to getting it,
too.

ancestors

I look forward to the day
when I will meet my ancestors
and they will tell me about their lives.

"I grew up in the coldest part of Finland and
survived on reindeer meat. For fun, we jumped
in a freezing lake before running to the sauna."

"I lived in England and lost my family to the
plague, but I eventually married a nice man who
still had most of his teeth."

"I traveled across the plains in a handcart
company with just one pair of shoes. It was the
hardest thing I'd ever done, but my family and I
grew closer than ever."

And they will look at me expectantly
and ask me to tell them about
life in 2024
and I will unsuccessfully
try to explain TikTok

sleeping in a snowstorm

This week of snowy rest
has been a tender mercy for
my pregnant self
But I know that I am privileged.

My mind keeps drifting
to all those on the street corners
who hold up signs,
the ones with their bright blue tents
set up precariously by the freeway

Where are they sleeping tonight?

Thoughts and prayers don't do much
to keep you warm
when it's 8 degrees outside.

Why in a country of billionaires
do we still have people that
must sleep on concrete
in the middle of a snowstorm?

the cherry speaks

It's me, hi
I'm the problem, it's me

I'm just the
size of a cherry

You vomit round the clock
I promise it'll be worth it later

It must be exhausting
being a full time baby incubator

hurkle-durkle

Today, I celebrated my Scottish heritage
and engaged in some
hurkle-durkling

(Lest you think I invented the term,
I learned it today via Facebook
so it must be real)

According to a meme
posted to Facebook
by a friend
whose name and picture
I don't actually recognize,
to hurkle-durkle
is a 200-year-old Scottish term
meaning "to lounge in bed long after it's time to
get up".

So,
it is only fitting
that I honor my ancestral clan
with a nice long
hurkle-durkle
on this snowy morning.

boot prints in the snow

There are tiny boot prints
cascading across the snow
in the driveway.

My own steps pause
to look at those pint-sized impressions.
I can't help but smile at
the way they zig zag erratically,
remembering the way you giggled gleefully
as you ran around stomping snow.

I never could have guessed
that I would find such joy
in snowy little boot tracks
or slobbery kisses
or syrupy finger hugs.
Never knew how it would
make me smile
to see four forgotten cars lined up in the
windowsill,
placed by tiny but intentional hands,
or how I would laugh
to reach under my pillow and discover
some trinket you'd loved and left for me.

"Will I love him?"
I asked almost daily
when you were still growing inside me,
terrified that God had left out
some important maternal instinct
when I was formed
and I'd be the sole woman in the world
who would have no connection to the
puny sluglike thing I'd created

But when they put you on my chest
for the briefest of instants
before whisking you away,
the world tipped
and I knew
nothing would ever be the same

You were mine,
flesh of my flesh
and I loved you instantaneously.

I knew
and yet I had no idea.

No idea how I would come to cherish
those soft little cheeks
and bright blue eyes,
the way you ask to "zoop up" your coat
and try to sweet talk us into more treats.

Never fathomed
the way hearing your small voice say
"I love you Mommy"
would mean more than any other words
ever uttered before.

"Will I love him?"
Yes, yes, you will
More than you have ever loved before.
Your heart will nearly burst from trying to
contain the immensity of what you feel for that
tiny, toddling human.

My heart bursts now as I remember.

The snow is already starting to melt,
taking your tracks with it,
and soon those boots will be far too small
and you will be far too big.

I look once more at those small snowy steps
before returning inside,
where I will squeeze you close
and breathe in the smell of your hair
as I try to keep a piece of this day with me
forever.

"Will I love him?"
If only you knew.

Wrap-Around Porch (from the Archives)

(Author's note: This is another "found" poem, although not from my college years. This was written in 2016 after going on a date with a very nice boy who told me his dream in life was to have a house with a wrap-around porch.)

Who am I to dismiss someone else's dreams?
I know firsthand how much it hurts
when someone scoffs at your ambitions.

You want to be Miss America? Ha.
You think you can be an actress? Please.
YOU, start a business? Are you kidding?
Why do you want to see the world? What's
wrong with right here?

And I hate the feeling of your dreams being
chipped away
One fleck at a time
Until all that's left of your glittering wish
is a tarnished lump that no longer resembles
hope.
Instead it whispers only
"practical." "realistic." "sensible."

Maybe your dreams were like that once.
Maybe you once dreamed of owning a castle
or an amusement park
or a spaceship
or a cottage by the sea
or even a bakery

But that shiny dream fell into the wrong hands
Those hands chipped away at it, smoothed down
the wild edges
And gave it back to you wrapped in crumpled
tissue paper
and stamped with the word 'ATTAINABLE.'

And that's why when someone --
when I--
ask you to tell me your dreams,
all you can muster is, "A wrap-around porch."

That is your wildest dream.
A house with a wrap-around porch.

I slowly nod.
A house with a wrap-around porch is
practical. realistic. sensible. attainable.

You'll fulfill that dream.

And who am I to scoff? It's your dream. I don't
want to chip it down anymore.

But I want you to know
that you could have told me.
You could have told me how that
roughly-handled little lump of wish originally
looked,
if it had been a castle or a sailboat or a house on
Mars.

I'm sure I would have loved it.
Attainable or not.
I would have smiled at the gleam in your eye as
you shared your secret wishes.
I would have told you to go for it.
Sensible or not.

I refuse to be one of those who diminishes
wishes.
I will smile and nod and tell you what a nice
goal.

But secretly I will pray that you remember how
to dream again.
I will pray that you dream big.
I will pray that you learn how to act on those
dreams
and I will pray

that one day you find your castle
and that it has the most beautiful
wrap-around porch

lumps

They sent in
a man
to talk to me about
my breasts.
He barely looked at me
as he discussed them like they were
lifeless lumps,
specimens to be prodded,
rather than the
life-giving vessels
that nursed and nourished
my baby for two years.
The words
"mass" and
"biopsy"
are scary words to hear,
but they sound almost
innocuous
in his monotone voice.
"It's probably benign,"
he points out,
finally looking up from his notes
to acknowledge the
living woman
with living breasts
sitting in front of him.

Well, okay then, I guess.

I retreat to the dressing room
and throw off the
horrible flimsy mauve fabric
that barely covered me
while attempting to tamp down
the icy lump of fear
threatening to disrupt
my calm demeanor.

The words
"mass" and "biopsy"
are still scary
especially when you're only 33
and 10 weeks pregnant
no matter how nonchalantly
you say them

"It's probably benign."
I repeat the words of the man
like a mantra.

On the way out,
I buy a $2 chapstick
for breast cancer research.
For good karma.
Just in case.

I really hope next time they
send a woman.

potty training

We are potty training
(I think it's for real this time).
Every 20 minutes or so,
my nearly 3-year-old yells out
"I need to go potty!"
and I stop what I'm doing
and we trek up the stairs
to the bathroom with the red car potty,
pull down pants
and wait while he sits
until he has squeezed out a tiny piddle
so he can watch two minutes
of his favorite annoying YouTube channel
which he fondly refers to as "mixers."
And every time he jumps up and yells
"I did it!"
(usually with a few stray drops dripping onto the
bath mat)
I turn on my most excited cheerleader voice
and celebrate with him.
I know we'll be back here before too long
and he'll be just as excited for that tiny pee
puddle
and I will cheer again
as if it is the very first time.

It boggles my mind that this was once me
sitting on my blue potty chair,
carrying it around the house with me,
equally excited for every little drop of pee
that I managed to squeeze out.
(There was no YouTube then. I was motivated
by the chalky taste of Smarties.)
And my Mother probably turned on her
cheerleader voice,
whooping excitedly as I danced around naked ,
wondering how long this potty training thing
would take
and how many more times she would have to
cheer me on
and clean up my piddles.

I wonder if our Heavenly Parents feel this way,
too;
if the tiny achievements we are proud of
are like tiny little pee puddles to them,
so inconsequential in their omnipotent eyes
but so exciting to our mortal minds.
And I'm sure they cheer for us
and smile fondly
as they wait
patiently
for the day when we will
finally graduate
to wearing big boy underwear.

prozac

My mother-in-law's
husky
is on Prozac.

And if that doesn't
sum up life in
January 2024
then I don't know what does.

a love story

Once we'd spend all night
talking until 3 AM,
dreading the moment when we'd say goodnight
and I'd make the
lonely trek
back to my
own apartment.

I got butterflies on those first nights,
reveling in the sparks that leapt
whenever your hand brushed mine.

Our nights look different now.
We wrestle a toddler into
spaceship jammies
then catch each other's eyes
and sigh, exhausted.
I retreat to the bathtub
You retire to your computer
And we're in bed by 10:30 pm sharp.

The butterflies have migrated elsewhere
and your beard is now
peppered with gray,

but when I catch your eye across the room,
you've never been more attractive.

Romance novels have glamorized
late night chats
and staying up exploring each other's bodies
until dawn.
(Any they definitely don't mention toddler
poop.)
But somehow they can never capture how six
years of loving and learning together have
amplified those sparks,
have taken what was once just attraction
and solidified it into
trust
commitment
joy
laughter
and all the other words
that don't quite encapsulate
six years of inside jokes
and knowing each other outside and in.

This is the love story I want.
10:30 bedtimes and a bathtub filled with cars
and living and laughing with you
until we don't have a single brown hair left.

Final Thoughts

For 21 days,
I have collected my thoughts,
Trying to capture
These fleeting snapshots

Of prints in the snow,
Of the hospital gown,
Of the muffled silence
As the snow came down,

Pregnancy pains,
And toddler firsts,
Days when I rested
And when I felt my worst.

These words may not be perfect
But they are mine.
I see life reflected
In each little line.

And I hope that something
That I've written rings true
For those that peruse
A page or two

And that maybe you'll realize
You're not so alone,
That some thought I've shared
Will help you feel known.

So while it is scary
To share a piece of my heart,
To send these words to a world
That may tear them apart,

I'm taking this chance,
With the start of this year,
And offer you these words,
With my love most sincere.

yours,
kelli